© **Wonderful Quotes For One And All**
BY SANDEEP RAVIDUTT SHARMA

Humble approach and caring attitude can go a long way in closing the deal in time.

© **Wonderful Quotes For One And All**
BY SANDEEP RAVIDUTT SHARMA

Sincerity and goodness mostly go together.

© **Wonderful Quotes For One And All**
BY SANDEEP RAVIDUTT SHARMA

Give special attention and care to those for whom you are the world and not the other way round. Celebrate each moment of your life including your failures. No doubt this would take time to put this in practice, but give it a try again and again.

© **Wonderful Quotes For One And All**
BY SANDEEP RAVIDUTT SHARMA

The seeker of truth will always have questions for you. So don't get irritated by their queries as it would help them to unveil and understand the truth well.

© **Wonderful Quotes For One And All**
BY SANDEEP RAVIDUTT SHARMA

The time never meets anyone for more than a second. If you forgot to act, you would lose out. Take the right action at the most appropriate time.

You can build a lot of external defences for your safety and security. But still, you may lose or die someday. Instead of working on externalities, it's wise to work on building or scaling your inner defences by following the righteous path including all aspects of life be it your health, food, exercise, spirituality, humour, meditation, calmness and kindness. If everything sounds complex just practice humanity.

Wonderful Quotes For One And All

© Wonderful Quotes For One And All
BY SANDEEP RAVIDUTT SHARMA

Brick by brick a house is constructed. Step by step involving your heart, love and compassion you can build your home.

Don't accept anything on their face value. Challenge the premise of your belief. Also, remember what is valid today may not remain valid forever.

© **Wonderful Quotes For One And All**
BY SANDEEP RAVIDUTT SHARMA

Shine like the sun. Let the light of your kindness and good work spread to one and all. Don't hide your good deeds and noble thoughts. The more you share these, the better is the effect.

© **Wonderful Quotes For One And All**
BY SANDEEP RAVIDUTT SHARMA

Don't let your mind rust by accepting word to word what others say. Mind your Mind in the right direction.

When a child throws a ball in the Sky, it is evident that it has to return back to the ground. But it may happen that a pair of hands catch it in mid-air. Our destiny also follows this rule, when we face challenges and are about to crash down, suddenly divine hands arrest our crash and make you land smoothly. Believe in the creator, and he will not let you fall.

© Wonderful Quotes For One And All
BY SANDEEP RAVIDUTT SHARMA

© Copyright 2018 Sandeep Ravidutt Sharma - All rights reserved.

In no way is it legal to reproduce, duplicate, or transmit any part of this document in either electronic means or in printed format. Recording of this publication is strictly prohibited and any storage of this document is not allowed unless with written permission from the publisher. All rights reserved. The information provided herein is stated to be truthful and consistent, in that any liability, in terms of inattention or otherwise, by any usage or abuse of any policies, processes, or directions contained within is the solitary and utter responsibility of the recipient reader. Under no circumstances will any legal responsibility or blame be held against the author / publisher for any reparation, damages, or monetary loss due to the information herein, either directly or indirectly. The author own all copyrights.

Legal Notice:
This book is copyright protected. This is only for personal use. You cannot amend, distribute, sell, use, quote or paraphrase any part or the content within this book without the consent of the author or copyright owner. Legal action will be pursued if this is breached.

Disclaimer Notice:
Please note the information contained within this book is for motivational, educational and knowledge sharing purpose only. Every attempt has been made to provide the reader accurate, up to date and reliable complete information. No warranties of any kind are expressed or implied. Readers acknowledge that the author is not engaging in the rendering of legal, financial, medical or professional advice. By reading this document, the reader agrees that under no circumstances the author / publisher is responsible for any losses, direct or indirect, which are incurred as a result of the use of information contained within this document, including, but not limited to, —errors, omissions, or inaccuracies.

If you have further questions, contact on
Tel: +919969256731
Email: sandeepraviduttsharma@gmail.com

© **Wonderful Quotes For One And All**
BY SANDEEP RAVIDUTT SHARMA

Dedication

This book is dedicated to **Goddess Bhairavi**. In the Hindu religion, the Goddess Bhairavi represents divine anger and wrath which is directed towards impurities within us as well as to the negative forces that obstructs our spiritual growth. Bhairavi Mata is also called as **Shubhamkari** and does good things. She is often depicted in images as holding a book, rosary and making abhaya and varada mudra with her hands. She is fiercely protective, lending us wisdom and power, steadiness and clarity. She personifies light and fire, supporting us to reveal what we keep hidden and inviting us to explore our hidden mind and any secret darkness.
 I hereby recite the following Bhairavi mool mantra...
"Om Hreem Bhairavi Kalaum Hreem Svaha"
And pray to **Goddess Bhairavi** for lending wisdom and power, steadiness and clarity in the life of my readers and the world. May Goddess Bhairavi protect us from negative forces along with removing impurities of our mind.

© **Wonderful Quotes For One And All**
BY SANDEEP RAVIDUTT SHARMA

Table of Contents

Introduction IV

Wonderful Quotes For One and All............................1

© Wonderful Quotes For One And All
BY SANDEEP RAVIDUTT SHARMA

Introduction

This book provides you with a list of **100 motivational quotes and thoughts** focussing mainly on improving your wellness quotient. Your positive attitude and happy mind can create a wonderful world. The positive thoughts can go a long way in helping you to find a way out of any complex situation. The encouraing words get etched on your mind creating and enhancing positive energy. I'm sure if you keeep reading, referring, sharing these thoughts and quotes, you may derive inspiration and develop a good understanding of various perspectives and facts of life.

"The words sound wonderful when you are listening and understanding its true meaning. Adopt the positive and wonderful words in your life, and be ready to climb the ladder of success."

I sincerely hope, you will find this book amazing, interesting, rejuvenating, unique and a constant source of inspiration.

Thank You and Happy Reading.

Your beliefs may influence your life. It's fine to have beliefs but not advisable to go for them blindly.

Run for life and not from life.

Close the gap between what you know and what you should, through learning in time.

© **Wonderful Quotes For One And All**
BY SANDEEP RAVIDUTT SHARMA

Share positive vibes and thoughts with one and all. Try to leave out all the negativity of your talks and focus on discussing the positive aspects.

© **Wonderful Quotes For One And All**
BY SANDEEP RAVIDUTT SHARMA

Helping someone known to you is generally what we do. Helping a stranger in troubled times can be the epitome of kindness. Be kind to one and all.

© **Wonderful Quotes For One And All**
BY SANDEEP RAVIDUTT SHARMA

The world rejoices for you, only when you win. Let's make winning a habit.

© **Wonderful Quotes For One And All**
BY SANDEEP RAVIDUTT SHARMA

When you look for greater rewards, you never know the rewards may come looking for you.

Your words can build or break trust. Trust is lost within a minute the moment you utter words not liked by the other. Build trust by sharing good words liked by one and all.

© **Wonderful Quotes For One And All**
BY SANDEEP RAVIDUTT SHARMA

One cannot board more than one train at the same time. Our choice decides our destiny.

Great leaders inspire others to become great.

© **Wonderful Quotes For One And All**
BY SANDEEP RAVIDUTT SHARMA

Be brave to lift the fallen, when you hear someone crying for help and see stone faces all around.

Don't just read the best things to do in life, but give a shot to do them in time.

© **Wonderful Quotes For One And All**
BY SANDEEP RAVIDUTT SHARMA

Be serious when it's matter of life and death and everything depends on your critical support.

Those who walk or run on an escalator are really in a hurry to reach their destination but surely are a risk to other people on board. Beware of such souls, or they may be responsible for your free fall.

Difficult times often make you stronger. In case you are facing such days let's pray to the Lord for you, asking for more patience, blessings and smooth passage through this dark tunnel. Remember glowing and welcoming light awaits you on the other side of this tunnel. Keep going.

© **Wonderful Quotes For One And All**
BY SANDEEP RAVIDUTT SHARMA

Trust connects people in a relationship.

Look for the best even among the worst, and you can find it soon.

© **Wonderful Quotes For One And All**
BY SANDEEP RAVIDUTT SHARMA

Thanks to Mother Nature for showering choicest blessings at every nook and corner of our life path. Smiling trees and flowers make our day. Greener grass cushions our tired legs and creates a soothing effect.

Change is inevitable. Those who don't change with time become history.

You can pretend to ignore the words but not what it means to you.

Once your life purpose is clear, fix a timeframe to achieve it.

© **Wonderful Quotes For One And All**
BY SANDEEP RAVIDUTT SHARMA

Find ways to keep your head high above the sea of stress and pain. Navigate with your will power to the shore of happiness and wave the ship of hope.

Write or riot...Choice is yours.

© **Wonderful Quotes For One And All**
BY SANDEEP RAVIDUTT SHARMA

A good human is one who feels content when the last loaf of bread available is given to his neighbour instead of him. Be human and we can make a better world to live.

© **Wonderful Quotes For One And All**
BY SANDEEP RAVIDUTT SHARMA

Fortunate ones are those who are blessed by the Sunshine of efforts and heartful of kindness. They are the ones who emerge victorious against the challenges of life and serve humanity with ease.

God has nominated you to fulfill the good wishes of many. It's your duty to uplift the fallen souls from the ground of darkness and help them fly in the beautiful and illuminating Sky.

Don't just walk away before you give a try. It's better to be a player rather than sit in the audience.

© **Wonderful Quotes For One And All**
BY SANDEEP RAVIDUTT SHARMA

At times one should watch the world and benefit from the change of perspective.

© **Wonderful Quotes For One And All**
BY SANDEEP RAVIDUTT SHARMA

You just can't hold the sun for quite long in your palm. It's just an illusion, come out of it and face the fact. Almost everyone in this Universe draws power from the Sun. It's time to thank Sun God for illuminating our world with the warm and daily blessings of sunshine.

The day you start assuming that you are the creator or the doer, ego takes over and would surely drive you down on the path of fire and thorns. Whatever you do surrender it to the Lord and you are on the path of enlightenment.

© **Wonderful Quotes For One And All**
BY SANDEEP RAVIDUTT SHARMA

Run after your goals in life with a plan of action and a timetable. Pursue them with single point focus and harnessing the power of your strong mind.

Humility builds a bridge to negotiate for a win-win situation.

© **Wonderful Quotes For One And All**
BY SANDEEP RAVIDUTT SHARMA

Time doesn't like to go back even if you want to revisit your past. Keep pace with the time if you can.

Going forward is less costly and more interesting compared to turning back and exploring again.

© **Wonderful Quotes For One And All**
BY SANDEEP RAVIDUTT SHARMA

Do things with conviction and leave no room for regret.

Success always trains the hopeful.

One gets hurt when people take you for granted and don't respect you for your individuality.

Not everyone would really know what you are thinking unless you tell them. Express yourself and you can find the right way.

© **Wonderful Quotes For One And All**
BY SANDEEP RAVIDUTT SHARMA

The ocean of joy is for those who live in the present.

© **Wonderful Quotes For One And All**
BY SANDEEP RAVIDUTT SHARMA

You don't have to react against every action of the interacting person. Sometimes silence creates a better impact than your choice of words.

© **Wonderful Quotes For One And All**
BY SANDEEP RAVIDUTT SHARMA

Those who are digging for Gold, don't bother about the depth of the mine.

© Wonderful Quotes For One And All
BY SANDEEP RAVIDUTT SHARMA

Little things in life matters the most and can make your life joyful.

© Wonderful Quotes For One And All
BY SANDEEP RAVIDUTT SHARMA

Run when you are in the race and not when you face life challenges.

© **Wonderful Quotes For One And All**
BY SANDEEP RAVIDUTT SHARMA

Once you believe that you are the greatest gift of God to mankind. You are sure to give your best to prove it to the world.

Obstacles appear in your path the moment you start focusing on your destination without paying due attention to your next step forward.

Go on a vacation if you have successfully completed your commitments.

Toughest situation gives birth to the greatest moments.

Get rid of jealousy if you want to be happy.

© **Wonderful Quotes For One And All**
BY SANDEEP RAVIDUTT SHARMA

If you can't stand in a queue, at least don't attempt to break in.

Check the time once and take a pause. Check again and the time has moved farther. You can't keep pace with the running time. But you can very well set and manage the distance between you and the time.

© **Wonderful Quotes For One And All**
BY SANDEEP RAVIDUTT SHARMA

Mental strength even scores high in a physical combat. Train your mind with the rightful thoughts and you can make it strong.

© **Wonderful Quotes For One And All**
BY SANDEEP RAVIDUTT SHARMA

Rising in life by putting someone down cannot last long. Follow your dreams, have self-belief and you can rise in life on your strengths.

© **Wonderful Quotes For One And All**
BY SANDEEP RAVIDUTT SHARMA

The feeling of love and togetherness is wonderful and amazing. All you need is trust and care at both ends.

Knowledge alone cannot ensure success unless you have the wisdom to apply it in time.

© **Wonderful Quotes For One And All**
BY SANDEEP RAVIDUTT SHARMA

Sometimes blood relations act as strangers and strangers act as friends and family. Choosing happiness is all in your mind. You can choose to remain unhappy because your own blood ignored you or find happiness with those who are not related but still love and care for you. Value the bond and not just the blood in a relationship.

© **Wonderful Quotes For One And All**
BY SANDEEP RAVIDUTT SHARMA

Be the change...not the smaller types...but significant change

© **Wonderful Quotes For One And All**
BY SANDEEP RAVIDUTT SHARMA

Each one of us is gifted with unique skills to earn our living. Some of us really do more than what one should. Appreciate the efforts to earn a living.

© **Wonderful Quotes For One And All**
BY SANDEEP RAVIDUTT SHARMA

Your competency helps you to choose your challenges, and emerge victorious each time.

© **Wonderful Quotes For One And All**
BY SANDEEP RAVIDUTT SHARMA

It's the arrogance of knowing everything that eludes one from learning more.

Those who wish to explore the purpose of their life ultimately finds it within.

© **Wonderful Quotes For One And All**
BY SANDEEP RAVIDUTT SHARMA

Standing tall is what the leader does, whether or not he gets the support.

The world is biased in favour of the achievers.

Blessings accumulated through kindness never get lost. It protects you every minute and ensures safe passage in hard times.

© **Wonderful Quotes For One And All**
BY SANDEEP RAVIDUTT SHARMA

Effective leadership comes from setting the right priorities and ensuring compliance.

© **Wonderful Quotes For One And All**
BY SANDEEP RAVIDUTT SHARMA

Let the world hear your laughter and compete with you. Laugh out the stress and laugh in the calmness.

Change is inevitable. Don't run away from change. Embrace it joyfully.

© **Wonderful Quotes For One And All**
BY SANDEEP RAVIDUTT SHARMA

Wait and watch when you don't know the next act.

The road divider helps you to drive safely. Likewise, certain dividers in your life like the distinction between work and personal life can help you in living peacefully.

Sacrifice smaller things in life to achieve bigger goals.

© **Wonderful Quotes For One And All**
BY SANDEEP RAVIDUTT SHARMA

As you walk, each of your foot keeps following the other and take you to the destination. The consistency of your actions with the appetite to improve can take you to places.

© **Wonderful Quotes For One And All**
BY SANDEEP RAVIDUTT SHARMA

Share and strengthen your bond with others and you can serve humanity with kindness. Be the one who leads in style or follows with discipline.

God is all powerful and has given you the power to choose what is right for you. Use this quality to take the right decision and make the most out of your life.

Be the role model you have been seeking for life.

Committing errors doesn't make you weak but repeating those errors every now and then definitely showcases your weak persona. Treat errors as lessons and take a vow to never repeat them again.

© **Wonderful Quotes For One And All**
BY SANDEEP RAVIDUTT SHARMA

Hesitation kills execution which is critical to your win. You can win only when you act.

© **Wonderful Quotes For One And All**
BY SANDEEP RAVIDUTT SHARMA

Keep going even if thousands of thorns are placed in your life path. No gain without pain applies to most of the success stories. It's all up to you how you tackle the thorns. Some may pick them up and throw in the fire, while others may wear an iron shoe and crush these thorns beyond recognition.

Do not pretend that you can hide the truth for long. Truth reveals itself to the world sooner or later. Seek the truth and it can empower you.

The struggle of life begins every morning. Be ready to find ways today to face the challenges again and emerge as a winner.

© **Wonderful Quotes For One And All**
BY SANDEEP RAVIDUTT SHARMA

Face the crowd or you become the crowd.

Do things with passion and total involvement.

Whatever you ask with a pure heart, you are bound to receive.

The world is not enough for those who dream of building a home in space.

Instead of finding inner calm try to build it.

Attract positive thoughts and emotions in your life.

Certain people are happy when you follow their rules and wishes. Follow what your heart says, and happiness is close by.

Thoughts come and go. All this is healthy if there is a break and you relax your mind in between. If the flow of thoughts doesn't stop and goes in a loop, it is quite dangerous as it gives birth to twin dragons...anxiety and depression. Avoid overthinking.

If one loses money, it can be earned again. But if one loses his/her character, it cannot be restored again.

© **Wonderful Quotes For One And All**
BY SANDEEP RAVIDUTT SHARMA

Run on rain? Don't run away when it's raining problems for you. Look for a cover by requesting your near and dear ones. If this doesn't work get ready to become wet in the ocean of sorrow without losing the hope of Sunrise. Pray to the Lord with the open heart and seek his blessings. That's the ultimate solution to dispel all your fears and strengthen your faith further.

© **Wonderful Quotes For One And All**
BY SANDEEP RAVIDUTT SHARMA

The seeker of truth sometimes gets destroyed in the process, but he may still become an inspiring torch for others who would complete his mission.

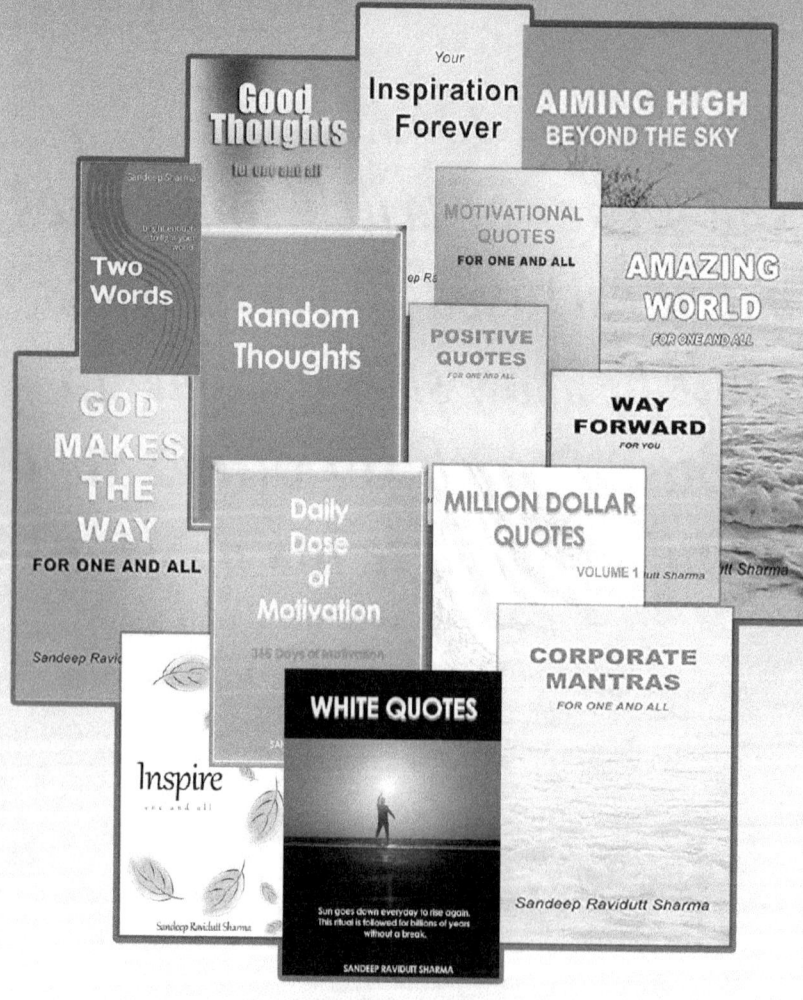

www.ingramcontent.com/pod-product-compliance
Lightning Source LLC
Chambersburg PA
CBHW070804220526
45466CB00002B/534